# Praise for FLIP IT®

*I just wanted to tell you how much I love FLIP IT! It's absolutely amazing, and I'm passionate about teaching it to the daycare providers I work with. It's simple, yet extremely effective. The acronym helps providers think straight and remember what to do in the midst of frustration. It's the best method I've learned since I started teaching in the '80s. FLIP IT is easy but makes me more creative when listing prompts. One more thing that's fun to know is that my eight-year-old daughter can FLIP: She understands it, knows what she's doing, and can FLIP you faster than you know what hit you! I always tell my providers that if my eight-year-old can do it, they can too!*

Amy Anderson, Professional Development Associate,
Project REACH, University of Missouri

*I just finished my very first FLIP IT training. The teachers involved are veteran preschool teachers, and they were challenged to think about how they were responding to children. I felt like we had many "lightbulb" moments as we discussed feelings, the use of "buts" when identifying feelings, and making inquiries for children. As they were challenged to think outside the box, they persevered, and their desire to use the strategies was evident. . . I cannot thank you enough.*

Pam Hamon, Special Services Specialist, Head Start, Richland, WA

*WOW. I am still FLIP IT crazy…We continue to brag on it every chance we get. It is so important to us and the children we serve.*

Sunni Zimmer, Mental Health and Disabilities Coordinator,
CAPE-Head Start/Early, Evansville, IN

*I have been using it with my four- and eight-year-olds with a lot of success— even this morning when my four-year-old was upset because she could not find her blanket. It was cool to see her think through the process and find the solution on her own, later asking me, "Daddy, are you happy that I am using my manners and not having a fit over my blankie?" Thank you for making my life a little easier!*

Ken Baker, Special Counselor and Dad,
Devereux Kanner Center, West Chester, PA

# FLIP IT!®

## Transforming
## Challenging Behavior

Four supportive steps to help young children
learn about their feelings, gain self-control,
and reduce challenging behavior

Rachel Wagner, MSW
with the Devereux Center for Resilient Children

Devereux Center for Resilient Children
Villanova, PA

Kaplan Early Learning Company
Lewisville, NC

© 2011 The Devereux Foundation

Published by Kaplan Early Learning Company

ISBN number 978-0-88076-749-1

Item number 22603

Printed in the United States of America.

For more information on the Devereux Center for Resilient Children,
call 1-866-872-4687.
www.CenterForResilientChildren.org

Devereux Advanced Behavioral Health is one of the nation's largest nonprofit organizations providing services, insight, and leadership in the evolving field of behavioral healthcare. Founded in 1912 by special-education pioneer Helena Devereux, the organization operates a comprehensive national network of clinical, therapeutic, educational, and employment programs and services that positively impact the lives of tens of thousands of children, adults, and their families every year. The Devereux Center for Resilient Children (DCRC) focuses on research-based prevention initiatives that help children develop resilience and strong social and emotional health.

## Disclaimer

The original FLIP IT® training curriculum was developed with the support of a one-year innovative grant from the New York State Office of Children and Family Services received by the Franziska Racker Centers (FRC). FRC is a not-for-profit dedicated to creating opportunities for people with special needs in the Ithaca, NY, area. FRC and the Devereux Center for Resilient Children are partners in ongoing efforts to enhance and expand FLIP IT® resources and training. FLIP IT® is a registered trademark of The Devereux Foundation.

The opinions, results, findings and/or interpretation of data contained herein are the responsibility of the Franziska Racker Centers and the Devereux Center for Resilient Children and do not necessarily represent the opinions, interpretation, or policy of the Office of Children and Family Services or the State of New York. The State of New York, the Office of Children and Family Services, and the United States Department of Health and Human Services have a right to a royalty-free, non-exclusive, and irrevocable license to reproduce, publish, distribute, or otherwise use, in perpetuity, any and all copyrighted or copyrightable material resulting from this agreement or activity supported by this agreement.

# FLIP IT®

**FLIP IT is a four-step supportive strategy to help young children learn about their feelings, gain self-control, and reduce challenging behavior.**

The FLIP IT guide teaches adults how to respond positively to everyday challenges and challenging behaviors in children ages three to eight. The guide walks teachers and families through the four FLIP IT steps in an easy-to-read format. Symbols and pictures make it easier to remember the steps. As you study, write your thoughts in the reflection boxes and use the photos of challenging scenarios to practice your FLIP IT responses.

FLIP IT workshops are offered online or in a classroom setting. For more information, contact the Devereux Center for Resilient Children at 1-866-TRAINUS or www.moreflipit.org.

# Contents

# Acknowledgments

**We wish to thank the many people who supported the development of this guide:**

The Devereux Center for Resilient Children team of Linda Likins, Susan Damico, Debi Mahler, Nefertiti Bruce, Debbie Alleyne, Caroll Berridge, Paul LeBuffe, and Martha Lindsay, who served as creative and organizational beacons.

The team at Racker, consisting of Roger Sibley, Dan Brown, Jody Scriber, Perri LoPinto, Tammy Goddard, Sue Budney, Jessica Jones, Linda Kline, and many others who supported FLIP IT's birth and growth.

Derry Koralek, editor extraordinaire, who helped transform FLIP IT from a training resource into a book.

Karen Cairone, who lent her passion for the strategy to her editing of the content and also wrote the wonderful suggestions in the appendices.

Kristin Tenney-Blackwell, research guru and author of the literature review.

The Kindness Project Team of Rochelle Giametta, Christine Peters, and Sarah Sedar, who pioneered the early childhood mental health cause and played a part in the evolution of FLIP IT.

Pilot-training participants and advisors, including Jeremy Aho, Gayle Cunningham, Mary Imbornone, Barbara Kaiser, Leslie Koplow, Amanda Lannie, Abbey Luterick, Joy Rowe, Connie Jo Smith, Tom Lottman, and Bob Wilcher, all of whom provided invaluable feedback.

The music team of Neil McIntyre and Larry Georgeson, who created the FLIP IT song that I use in training.

The children and dedicated families who helped promote positive approaches to addressing challenging behavior.

The original creative team of Tana Ebaugh as art director and graphic designer, Robert Kaussner as photographer, and Steve Carver as illustrator, for the original FLIP IT training materials.

Heather Beck, for being a natural "FLIP'er" before it ever had a name, and her daughter, Hailee, who is living proof that it works.

Kelly Jackson, Jan Laning, Megan Noonan, Carrie Perfetti, Holly Wilcher, and Kristen Kerr, whose friendship and enthusiasm nurtured me throughout this and many other life challenges.

The Wittmer family, who played a role in my fondest early childhood memories.

My Wagner family of Daniel, Shannon, Peyton, and Langston, who inspire me.

My mom and dad, who raised me to be a feeler and a thinker. True humanitarians and the original "FLIP'ers."

# Setting the Stage
# for **FLIP IT**

**"It's OK, honey. You're OK. Come on out and sit with me."**
**We may say these words to a child who is scared and has**
**crawled under a table. The tone and the sentiment are gentle**
and nurturing but do not help the child understand the emotions
that got her under the table in the first place. By beginning to understand the feelings that made her crawl under the table, she can
then learn to independently cope with those challenging feelings
in a healthier way. FLIP IT provides a simple way to help children
do this.

FLIP IT offers a strength-based, commonsense, and effective
four-step strategy. Adults can use FLIP IT when confronting a number of challenging behaviors, such as crawling under the table,
throwing toys, whining, spitting, or hitting peers. The four steps
embodied in the FLIP IT mnemonic include:

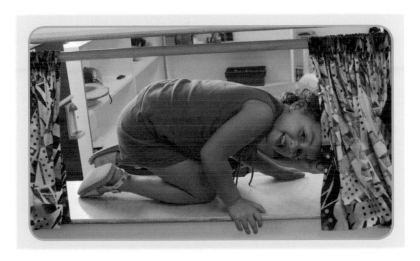

1. **FEELINGS**: Gently talk with the child about his feelings. Tell him what you see and hear as a result of his emotions. Help him to identify the root feelings causing the behavior.

2. **LIMITS**: Remind the child of the positive limits and expectations you have for his behavior. Loving and simple limits help surround children with a sense of consistency, safety, and trust.

3. **INQUIRIES**: Encourage the child to think about solutions to his challenges. Ask questions that promote problem-solving and healthy coping skills. Inquiries invite children to think, learn, and gain self-regulation.

4. **PROMPTS**: Provide creative cues, clues, and suggestions for the child who is having difficulty. Enthusiastic, bright ideas can lead the way to better problem-solving skills.

FLIP IT is best practiced by using all four steps in fairly quick succession (1–10 minutes from start to finish). Experienced FLIP IT users may find that only one or two steps are needed to resolve the situation.

FLIP IT incorporates best-practice approaches into a method that is easy to remember and applicable in a variety of challenging situations. FLIP IT may be used every day for minor challenges and conflicts with one child or with multiple children. FLIP IT also can be used as a targeted intervention intended to support the emotional growth of a child displaying specific behavioral concerns. FLIP IT requires consistency to bring about long-term change. Children who frequently experience the FLIP IT process become emotionally aware problem-solvers who develop healthy coping skills that will last a lifetime.

While FLIP IT is a versatile and portable strategy, it may not always be the best strategy for a given situation. FLIP IT can and should be integrated with effective strategies that support the development of positive relationships, emotional awareness, problem-solving skills, and healthy coping in children (and adults). Please note that the FLIP IT strategy requires time and consistency. It is not the magical answer for every challenging situation. FLIP IT, by itself, is not designed to resolve severe emotional and behavioral issues. In such cases, seek support from mental health professionals to establish a comprehensive plan that may include FLIP IT. Finally, FLIP IT considers the root causes of a child's behavior but does not center on the functional behavioral assessment process used by many mental health professionals.

## FLIP IT Began with Haley

As a preschool teacher, I noticed children's challenging behavior on the rise, and I felt discouraged that the strategies and techniques I had learned did not work. I was desperate for something that would help me with a young girl in my class who was beginning to keep me awake at night with worry. Haley had lived through a lot; she had been abused, placed in a shelter, expelled from several preschools for her violent behavior, and at the time lived in a foster home. On a typical day at preschool, she attacked other children, called me terrible names, kicked me in the shins, and told me I was fat, all while attempting to "rip my eyeballs out."

Haley's challenging behavior was clearly coming from a deep and emotionally hurt place.

I needed a strategy that would address not only the behaviors but the hurt behind them. With guidance from the Devereux Early Childhood Assessment (DECA) Program, the wisdom of early childhood leaders, and the suggestions of my very wise co-workers, friends, and family, my colleagues and I began consistently responding to Haley's challenging behavior with four simple steps. Our approach (now known as FLIP IT)

was rooted in the development of an empathic, trusting relationship. With that base, we were able to teach Haley about emotional awareness and support her development of emotional control through problem-solving and healthy coping skills.

Every time Haley tried to "rip my eyeballs out," I acknowledged her FEELINGS and then set a loving LIMIT. I would say, "Haley, I see you are getting so mad. Remember we agreed to keep each other safe here." Then I would INQUIRE to encourage problem solving ("What can we do to help you with your mad?") and PROMPT her with coping strategies ("Can we rub your back or squeeze some play dough?").

By consistently using the FEELINGS step, we helped Haley understand and identify the painful emotions that bubbled up inside her before she would lash out. Just like every adult, each child has to develop her own unique coping strategies. After some trial and error with INQUIRIES and PROMPTS, we found that foot scratching worked best to soothe Haley. After several months of using FLIP IT with consistency, Haley learned to identify her own emotions and would often rip off her socks and ask for a foot scratch instead of attacking children and teachers. Haley's foster parents supported her progress by using FLIP IT at home. Later they adopted Haley, who went to kindergarten with a back scratcher for her feet! Haley is now a young woman who has been well loved and supported, and while she will always struggle with the trauma from her early years, she has coping skills. For children like Haley, FLIP IT is just one of many strategies used as part of a much more comprehensive plan to support all their needs.

You will find that the FLIP IT strategy is not new. It takes all that is old, wise, and good and makes it easy to remember and use. This strategy is not about trying to control children like Haley but about teaching them to control themselves in the context of a loving and safe relationship.

Since my work with Haley, I have become a social worker and have shared the FLIP IT strategy with many teachers and families. I am excited to share FLIP IT with you, and I hope you find it a rewarding and helpful strategy.

# Resilience Theory and the FLIP IT Strategy

Resilience is the ability to bounce back from difficulty, misfortune, or change. The FLIP IT strategy helps children become resilient by teaching them how to cope in times of challenge. FLIP IT can be used as a stand-alone technique and/or as a strategy to enhance the implementation of the Devereux Early Childhood Assessment (DECA) Program, an assessment and planning system that measures and promotes protective factors in young children.

Three critical protective factors in the development of resilience in young children are attachment, initiative, and self-regulation. Attachment is the mutual, strong, and long-lasting relationship between a child and a significant adult, such as a parent, family member, or teacher. Initiative is the child's ability to use independent thought and action to meet his needs. Self-regulation is the child's ability to experience a range of feelings and express them using the words and actions that society considers appropriate. To be resilient and successful in school and life, children need to develop all three of these healthy protective factors. FLIP IT can be a powerful tool for supporting that process.

To learn more about resilience and how to promote protective factors in young children and the adults who care for them, visit www.centerforresilientchildren.org More information on the Devereux Center for Resilient Children is also found in Appendix E.

# Relationships and Empathy

Every strategy we use with children will only be as successful as the relationship it is built upon. We learn best from people who make us feel safe, valued, and understood. For a child, FLIP IT is the process of learning about feelings and healthy coping skills, and a caring adult must facilitate this learning. Strive every day to strengthen your relationship with the child through play, listening, respect, and caring. FLIP IT also can help strengthen the bond between you and the child, because the FEELINGS step conveys empathy, the ability to see and feel from another person's perspective. Seeing challenging situations through the eyes of the child is critical to the FLIP IT process. Even if the emotion or challenge seems small to you, try to imagine what it means to the child at his age, in his world, with his limited life experiences. Empathy while using FLIP IT means h0Noring a "child-size problem" for what it means to that child. Showing empathy to a child is the first step in teaching him to have empathy for others.

When we look through the eyes of a child, we notice what she feels as well as how she reacts to the people and environment around her. Sometimes a child's negative emotions are a direct result of something we can and should change about ourselves or the environment. Empathy helps us become more aware of the child and more aware of ourselves. Try to embrace the lessons empathy teaches. Teachers, parents, and caregivers do not always know what to do, and they often feel as though they have done the wrong thing. As you learn to use FLIP IT, you may find yourself feeling skeptical, guilty, overwhelmed, or frustrated. Try to be gentle with yourself on this journey, and take time to notice your own feelings.

In times of personal stress, try using FLIP IT on yourself first. Practice the four FLIP IT steps to improve your own emotional awareness and emotional control. This can make you a better FLIP'er and a happier person.

1. **FEELINGS**:  Notice what is happening inside you during times of stress, before you react. Ask yourself, "What am I really feeling?" Explore your emotions.

2. **LIMITS**:  Decide what the appropriate boundaries or limits are for the situation.

3. **INQUIRIES**:  Ask yourself, "What is the best way to handle this?"

4. **PROMPTS**: Use creative thinking if you have difficulty finding a solution. Ask a friend, family member, or colleague for suggestions to help you think outside the box.

Becoming aware of your feelings, knowing your limits, and using healthy coping skills to solve problems will help you on your personal journey, in your work with children, and in your relationships with other adults.

# A Child in Mind

As you read the FLIP IT guide, you may find it useful to have in mind one or more children you want to try the FLIP IT process on. Use the opportunities presented in this guide to jot down reflections about your particular situation.

As you prepare to use the FLIP IT strategy with a child, it is important to reflect on who he is, so that you may better empathize with his point of view during challenging times. Get a more complete view of the child by making regular observations of his behavior and consulting multiple sources of information (other adults, medical records, and so on). Take a moment to reflect on a particular child and write down his strengths and interests.

List the child's strengths:

_____

_____

_____

List the child's interests:

_____

_____

_____

What needs or challenges does the child present to you?
List the child's challenges:

_____

_____

_____

# ICK—What Causes Challenging Behavior?

ICK refers to the negativity or risk factors in an individual's life. ICK includes factors within ourselves, our families, and our environment that make us feel bad and less able to handle challenges. When you reflect on ICK in the life of a child, try to visualize it as a sticky and heavy slime that covers her and weighs her down. ICK sticks to us and makes coping with life's difficulties even more challenging. What factors may cause ICK in the life of the child or children you have in mind?

**Within Self (Internal) ICK:**
Examples: Low self-esteem, a learning disability

_____

_____

_____

**Family ICK:**
Examples: Divorce, financial stress

_____

_____

_____

**Environmental ICK:**
Examples: Violent TV, bullying at school

_____

_____

_____

When children react to the ICK in their lives, they often FLIP IN or FLIP OUT.

FLIP INs happen when feelings stay inside and are expressed with more self-destructive behavior. FLIP OUTs happen when the negative feelings come out in unhealthy or damaging ways. We all have ICK in our lives, and this does not mean we are doomed or sick. "ICKNESS" does not have to equal sickness, unless we choose unhealthy coping strategies that can become hurtful habits. The goal is to give children healthy ways to cope with ICK early in life, so that unhealthy options like drugs, alcohol, or negative relationships are less appealing as they get older.

First, list examples of FLIP IN behaviors you have seen in a child or children.

**FLIP INs:**
Examples: Hiding under a table, refusing to speak

_____

_____

_____

Healthy coping strategies that become overused can also be considered FLIP IN behaviors. For example, an adult may use jogging as a method to cope with stress, but if the jogging becomes an obsession that interferes with daily life and well-being, it has become a FLIP IN because it is no longer healthy. With children, FLIP INs are often easily ignored, but they still require adult attention to deal with the ICK that causes them. Also be aware that some FLIP IN behaviors may help a child gain positive and nurturing attention from adults. When a child learns that acting scared results in a kind and soothing response from adults, then a child who is needy for attention or attachment may frequently garner attention through these unhealthy means.

Now, list examples of FLIP OUT behaviors you have seen in a child or children.

**FLIP OUTs:**
Examples: Hitting, destroying toys

_____

_____

_____

FLIP OUT behaviors are more obvious and usually get more attention than FLIP IN behaviors. Some children's FLIP OUTs become a useful crutch because the behavior ends up working in their favor. FLIP OUTs often get a child what she wants both physically and emotionally. For example, if a child screams at the grocery store and gets a candy bar to be quiet, the child has learned that screaming (a FLIP OUT behavior) helps her to get what she wants. Many children use FLIP OUT behaviors because of ICK to receive more attention, more boundaries, and more time with the adults in their lives. FLIP IT can help you to provide all of these in a healthy way.

FLIP INs or FLIP OUTs can become bad habits. FLIP IT helps adults instill in children healthy coping strategies that can last a lifetime. We all strive for healthy habits, but just like children, we are always a work in progress, and self-reflection is important. Reflect a moment on your own ICK.

What is your environmental ICK?

_____

_____

What is your family ICK?

_____

_____

What is the internal ICK you carry?

_____

_____

Think about your coping habits. How do you respond to your ICK? Do you FLIP IN and hold it all inside? Describe.

_____

_____

Do you FLIP OUT and act in unhealthy ways? Describe.

_____

_____

How does your ICK affect the children around you?

_____

_____

Having healthy coping habits means that when times are full of ICK, we choose to stay calm and use FLIP IT (show self-regulation and problem-solving skills), rather than showing FLIP OUT or FLIP IN behaviors. When we use FLIP IT with children, they learn to stay calm, understand their emotions, set limits, and use healthy coping skills to solve problems. Teaching them to do this early in life develops healthy habits that will last a lifetime.

*Whenever Maya used to get upset, she would cope by running away and burying her head in her arms. This worked for her at age four, but I worried that as she got older, she would not face challenges with confidence. The FLIP IT strategy taught me that while it is OK for Maya to get upset, she needed my love and support to learn how to cope, rather than run away. It took some time, but I can tell that Maya now believes she can solve her own problems. She even seeks out challenges, just so she can overcome them!*
—Tyson, father of four-year-old Maya (Colorado)

# ♡ Step 1—FEELINGS

*Every time we go to the park and it is time to leave, he runs away from* me and I can't catch him. I yell at him. I threaten to take away television when we get home. I even try to bribe him with treats. Then I learned about Step 1, the FEELINGS step of FLIP IT, and I realized I never even thought about what Jeremy was feeling. I

just knew his running away was a problem for me. Instead of antici-pating things going wrong, I thought about the situation from his point of view and finally understood that leaving the park was hard for him. Jeremy really loves the park and was sad to leave. Under-standing his feelings and talking with him about them really helped us work together and overcome this challenge.

—Janice, mother of seven-year-old Jeremy (New Hampshire)

Begin the FLIP IT process with Step 1 FEELINGS. Gently talk with the child about his feelings and what you are seeing and hear-ing as a result of his emotions. Help the child identify the root feelings causing the behavior.

## Why Are FEELINGS Important?

Feelings are at the root of all behavior. When children have good feelings at their roots, positive behavior will grow like a healthy

13

tree. When behavior is negative, we must check the roots for ICK (negative influences or risk factors). Children do not always understand the negative feelings they experience or why they FLIP IN or OUT. Unhealthy or destructive behavior from children often gets big reactions from adults, who just want the behavior to stop. If we address the behavior without addressing the root feelings, the ICK will keep growing, and the negative behavior will reoccur. Instead, we need to gently talk with children about their feelings and what we see, hear, and experience as a result. Getting to the root cause of the behavior will lessen the ICK and support a child's ability to identify her emotions. Children must become aware of what they feel before we ask them to control it.

## What Are Some Common FLOPs with This Step?

A FLOP is when, despite our good intentions, we respond to challenging behavior in a way that does not help resolve the situation or encourage the child to gain self-regulation. It is normal to FLOP. When it happens, we need to give ourselves a break, then regroup for the next time.

Sometimes FLOPs happen when adults try to get to the root of the behavior by asking the child "Why?" Asking this may confuse children because they often do not understand why they behaved in a certain way. Young children tend to be impulsive. Asking "why" may lead a child to feel blamed, shamed, or defensive. It also implies that there might be a correct answer, but in the case of harmful or hurtful behavior, there is no acceptable answer that would explain why one child hurt another. Try replacing "why" questions about behavior to "what" questions: For example, rather than "Why did you do that?" try "What is happening inside you?" Please note that asking "why" for non-behavioral questions is still a great approach to encourage learning ("Why is the sky blue?" or "Why does the water run down the hill?")

FLOPs also happen when we respond to the first thing we see—the child's behaviors—instead of the child's feelings. Spontaneous responses like "Stop that," "Be nice," or "Put that down" do not lead to long-term solutions.

# Take Some Time to Reflect

1.   Imagine if you were feeling really sad and someone told you to smile.

   1.   Would you feel understood, comforted, or as though your feelings were validated?
      ☐Yes   ☐No
   2.   Would you feel like your troubles were instantly solved?
      ☐Yes   ☐No

   Imagine if you were feeling frustrated or tired and someone asked you, "Why aren't the dishes done yet?"

   1.   Would you feel understood, comforted, or as though your feelings were validated?
      ☐Yes   ☐No
   2.   Would you feel defensive?
      ☐Yes   ☐No

   In many ways throughout a day, we ignore feelings, especially unpleasant ones. Ignoring emotions will not lead to feeling understood, comforted, or validated, nor will it resolve problems.

2.   Have the behavioral strategies you have tried with children been successful? List the common strategies you have learned or tried.

   **Strategy:**
   Examples: Time out, relaxation techniques / breathing

   _____

   _____

Now ask yourself, did that strategy…
- help to strengthen your relationship with the child?
- address the root cause or the feelings behind the behavior?
- help the child learn how to control her emotions?
- help the child to become a problem-solver?
- help to make long-term changes in the child's behavior?

These questions help us determine if a strategy is accomplishing long-term goals and helping the child develop emotional awareness and control. Some strategies like FLIP IT help accomplish many, if not all, of the five objectives reflected in these questions, while others may not. Some common strategies may effectively bring about short-term changes (quick fixes) but do not support lifelong growth. Continue to use these strategies if they help you get through tough days as you develop your FLIP IT skills. Remember that no one strategy can do it all, and it is up to you to combine a variety of strategies that work for you and support growth in the child.

## How Do I Get Started with Step 1 FEELINGS?

- *Change a habit.* It may not be your first instinct to ask "What is he feeling?" as soon as a child acts out. Try coaching yourself to "go for feelings" every time you are faced with a child's challenging behavior.
- *Use some tools.* Use the practice pictures in this book, along with posters, stickers, bracelets, and so on, to help you get comfortable doing the FEELINGS step first.
- *Talk about all feelings.* Practice noticing and talking about feelings with a variety of people who are having all kinds of emotions, even happy ones. Use feelings books and social skills curriculum (for instance, the *Second Step®* curriculum) to enhance children's learning about feelings.
- *Keep it simple.* Young children likely have only a very basic vocabulary about feelings, so begin with simple feelings words (sad, mad, nervous, tired). Then expand the vocabulary once you and the child get the hang of it.

- *Just start.* You may begin using the FEELINGS step in your day-to-day life, even before you have learned the L, I, and P of FLIP IT.

### "What should I say?"

Below are sample lead-in phrases to address a child's feelings. They may come in handy when you are first learning to explore feelings with children. Choose some samples you like and then make them your own.

- "I see you are doing _____. I wonder if you are feeling _____."
- "Wow, it really looks like you are feeling _____."
- "I notice you are doing _____. What is going on inside?"
- "Your body is getting antsy. Are you feeling nervous?"
- "I'm sorry you are feeling so _____."
- "What are you feeling?"

## Practice Pictures

The following photos show children engaged in a variety of challenging behaviors. Use the photos to practice Step 1 FEELINGS. As you learn each new FLIP IT step, you will revisit these scenes and add to your responses. (Feel free to use creative license when interpreting the photos.) Sample responses appear in Appendix D.

**A child breaks crayons into pieces.**
- What would you say to address FEELINGS?

_____

_____

_____

**A child crawls under the table during transition time.**
- What would you say to address FEELINGS?

_____

_____

_____

**Children fight over the paintbrush.**
- What would you say to address FEELINGS?

_____

_____

_____

# Frequently Asked Questions About Step 1 FEELINGS

**1. What if there is immediate physical danger?**
The FEELINGS step can be completed in as little as 10 seconds, but if there is real danger, move directly to Step 2 LIMITS. Revisit FEELINGS once the crisis has been averted.

**2. What if the FEELINGS step sparks a discussion?**
Great! Use this as an opportunity to talk with the child about feelings. This may be all the child needs from you to help curb the behavior. There is no need to rush to the next steps if a child is ready and willing to talk.

**3. What if I don't know what the child is feeling?**
Try to describe what you are seeing and hearing from the child and guess what might be the underlying feeling (for example, "I see your face is getting red, and you are making growling sounds. I think you are feeling angry."). The act of trying to empathize is just as important for the adult (sometimes more important) than correctly labeling the feeling. The child will feel noticed and see you are reaching out. Imagine that during an exhausting day at work, your co-worker notices you dragging and rather than telling you to smile, she says, "You look sad." Even if she got your feeling wrong (you were not sad, you were tired), it means something to you that she cared. You can also simply ask, "What are you feeling?" or "What is happening inside you right now?"

**4. Should I start the FLIP IT process with a child who is out of control or having a tantrum?**
It is usually best to wait for a child who is having a tantrum to calm down before engaging in a discussion, but sometimes if a child is out of control, the FEELINGS step can be soothing. Use a calm tone of voice and validate the child's feelings. ("You are so angry. I can see from your tight fists how angry you are feeling.") If talking to the child seems to escalate the behavior, wait until the child is able to hear you.

**5. How do I get the child's attention in order to begin the FLIP IT process?**
Getting a child's attention is truly the first step in any effort to communicate. With young children, capturing their interest can often be done with some theatrics. Enthusiasm, changes in tone of voice (for example, whispering), facial expressions, and gestures can work to get a child's attention. Interesting noises (such as bells) and visual props (puppets, for example) are also useful. You may need to get closer to the child, get on her eye level, or gently touch her arm.

**6. What if the child is nonverbal or developmentally delayed?**
All children deserve and benefit from having their emotions acknowledged. Even if a child cannot respond, talk to him about feelings. It is important to narrate children's feelings and

experiences. Keep talking, even if he cannot or does not respond. Pictures, books, and toys that promote awareness of emotions can help both verbal and nonverbal children increase their feelings vocabulary. Some children may prefer to point to pictures rather than talk directly about their feelings. (See Appendix C.)

**7. What if I sound fake when I try to talk about feelings?**
When you are getting started, have a lead-in phrase that will work in most situations, such as, "Wow, it looks like you are feeling _____." Remember, less can be more. You don't need to say much; just say it with kindness. Make your FEELINGS statements suit your personal style—for example, "You are looking awfully mad," or "Girl, you look heated!" Both work!

**8. Can you use the FLIP IT steps with a room of children or more than one child at a time?**
Yes. When more than one child is engaging in the same behavior (for example, running around the room), they are probably feeling similar emotions (such as boredom), so go ahead and FLIP the group. (With enthusiasm, you might say, "Wow, I can see that my friends are getting wiggly and running all around. You all must be feeling bored with this story.") If there are multiple problem behaviors to address, it is best to start with the most dangerous behavior. Only you will know where you should begin. Use your best judgment, factoring in whether or not there are other adults nearby who can help.

**9. What if I come upon a situation where I do not know what has happened between two children? I have learned it is important to get the facts, so do I try to get the facts before I address FEELINGS?**
Exploring feelings helps you to get to the root of an issue, so in many cases, doing the FEELINGS step will help you get to the facts. With young children, the facts are often less important to the problem-solving process than you may think. Sometimes the fact-finding mission for a child becomes more about blame and punishment than about learning and growth. When teaching children to better cope during times of challenge, it matters less who had the toy first; the feelings that motivated the argument are more important.

Once a child knows the feeling, she can then problem solve a better way to cope in the future when she wants the toy. Popular problem-solving models that address facts first have proven to be very positive and effective, so please consider using a variety of strategies to meet all your needs.

**10. What if the child says, "No! That is not what I'm feeling!" or begins to mock me or pushes me away?**
Let this rejection lead to an open discussion about feelings. At the very least, you tried, and in doing so, you conveyed compassion. Some children might prefer to be alone with their ICK, and they will try to push you away with even more negative behaviors. Don't let them keep you away. No child should be alone with ICK for too long. Keep talking about feelings.

## Step 1 FEELINGS
## Promotes Resilience

Resilience is the ability to bounce back from difficulty, misfortune, or change. To be resilient and successful in school and life, children need to develop the three healthy protective factors: attachment, initiative, and self-regulation. Doing the FEELINGS step with children helps to strengthen all three of those factors. When children know that others kindly and calmly notice their feelings, they feel safe and supported, strengthening their attachment. Initiative is also strengthened during the FEELINGS step, because when children learn about their emotions, they also learn how to better act independently with confidence. Finally, the FEELINGS step strengthens children's self-regulation. When children gain emotional awareness, they begin to understand what is happening inside before they act out impulsively. Doing the FEELINGS step now provides benefits that last forever.

The FEELINGS step was inspired by a Devereux Center for Resilient Children (DCRC) resource that suggested identifying and empathizing with a child's point of view. For more information on the Devereux Center for Resilient Children resources and materials see Appendix E.

# ✋ Step 2—LIMITS

*As a new teacher, I was very hesitant to set limits and tell children "no." I was so busy and did not feel like I had time for the power struggles that came with limit setting, so I let things slide. Even when I tried and said things like, "We play with trucks on the floor, not in the air," no one would listen. My students were walking all over me, and my classroom felt chaotic and sometimes unsafe. I quickly was learning that I didn't have time to not establish limits, but I did not know how to follow through once they were set. FLIP IT taught me* that limits work best if you start out by validating the child's feelings. Limits are also easier to live with when followed by inquiries and prompts. Young children need help living within the loving boundaries we set, and FLIP IT helps children do just that.*

—Lana, Head Start teacher (Massachusetts)

Once you have talked with a child about what she is feeling, proceed when necessary to Step 2 LIMITS. Remind children of the positive limits and expectations you have for their behavior. Loving and simple limits help surround children with a sense of consistency, safety, and trust.

# Why Are LIMITS Important?

Children need to explore to learn. They must try new things, test out ideas, and challenge their endless imaginations. Sometimes all of that learning and exploring can lead to challenging behavior. Excited children can be impulsive and often will test limits. They may have emotions that cause them to act in inappropriate ways. Limits can help guide children toward healthy, safe, and positive behaviors and choices. Loving limits tell children what you expect, what behavior is acceptable, and how to stay safe ("We keep our cars driving on the floor" or "We keep each other safe"). Limits (or rules) are most successful when children are invited to help set them. Remind children regularly of the limits and expectations to prevent unsafe or challenging situations. When challenges do occur, talk about feelings and then remind the child of the positive limits and expectations you have for her behavior.

# What Are Some Common FLOPs with This Step?

Sometimes we FLOP when we tell children what they can't do, rather than helping them understand what they can or should do instead. Limits work best when they remind children of a positive expectation that can help them to move forward ("Remember, we agreed to use friendly words") versus a limit aimed at shutting down behavior without guidance as to what to do instead ("Stop being rude").

We may also FLOP if we do not regularly discuss, review, and remind children of the limits we have set. As adults, we generally try to follow the law because those laws were put in place to keep us safe. Sometimes the law (or limit) slips our mind (for instance, driving over the speed limit) and we need reminders. Speed limit signs every mile or so help to remind us of what is expected. Children also need reminders all along the way. Reviewing limits (expectations) with children regularly during times of calm will make reminders during times of crisis more meaningful.

# Take Some Time to Reflect

1. To be consistent with the limits you set, it is important to know where you stand on certain challenging behaviors and situations. You can FLIP most situations, but there will be some challenges you may decide are non-negotiable (not up for the FLIP IT discussion) and you are putting your foot down. There may also be times when you begin the FLIP IT process and realize that you are better off ignoring this behavior for the moment.

Reflect on situations where you will put your foot down rather than follow the FLIP IT steps in order.

Examples: Running in the road, playing with fire

_____

_____

_____

Also reflect on situations where the child does not show signs of a distressing emotion and is engaging in a non-harmful behavior that may be better off ignored.

Examples: Silly noises, twirling in an uncrowded store

_____

_____

_____

Remember, you can use the FLIP IT strategy in most situations so that the child can better understand his feelings and learn healthy coping skills. Consistency is important; therefore, discuss these lists with other adults in the child's life so that the child hears a consistent limit and knows expectations for his behavior.

2.    Limits work best when they remind children of a positive expectation or a behavior the child needs to learn. ("Remember, we use a strong voice when we ask for things we need.") Limits aimed at shutting down behavior without any guidance leave children confused about what they should do instead.

Practice rewriting the CAN'T statements below so that the child will know what she CAN do. Think about the behavior or skill the child needs to learn instead of the negative behavior she is choosing.

CAN'T LIMIT: "Stop running inside!"
CAN LIMIT: "Use your walking feet inside."

CAN'T LIMIT: "Stop whining."
CAN LIMIT: _____

CAN'T LIMIT: "Stop wrestling around."
CAN LIMIT: _____

Children respond better when they understand what is expected of them and they are included in setting those expectations.

# How do I get started with Step 2 LIMITS?

- *Make rules together.* Open a discussion about the rules with children. If they help you establish limits, they will feel more invested in sticking to them. You might be surprised how much they already know about acceptable behavior.
- *Keep it simple.* Try to stick to a few simple rules that fit a variety of situations (Rule 1 – We keep ourselves safe; Rule 2 – We keep each other safe; Rule 3 – We keep our things safe), so that you and the child are not confused.
- *Stick to it.* If you establish a rule, you must stick to it. Inconsistency breeds confusion, which can lead to testing. Work together with other adults to decide when to put your foot down, when to walk away, and when to FLIP IT.

- *Use some tools.* Use the practice pictures in this book along with your own reminder tools (posters, stickers, and bracelets) to help you get comfortable doing the LIMITS step.
- *Change a habit.* Setting limits that promote learning and positive expectations rather than telling the child "no" may challenge our natural habits, especially during a tough situation. Often the hardest part of setting limits is remembering to talk about feelings first.
- *Adjust when needed.* You may sometimes notice after you talk about FEELINGS that a LIMIT is not necessary, and you can stop the FLIP with F. Other times, you will need to quickly move on to INQUIRIES and PROMPTS to help the child live with the limit you've set.

## "What should I say?"

Below are sample lead-in phrases to address a child's feelings before quickly establishing a LIMIT. They may come in handy when you are first learning to FLIP IT. Choose some samples you like and personalize them.

- "I hear you saying unfriendly words. I wonder if you are feeling _____. We use friendly words here."
- "Wow, it really looks like you are feeling _____. We keep each other safe."
- "Your body is getting antsy. Are you feeling nervous? It's OK to feel nervous."
- "I'm sorry you are feeling so _____. We use gentle touches here."
- "I see you are excited about our visitor and you are running in the room. Our rule is to sit at circle."

# Practice Pictures

Revisit the following photos and add a LIMIT to your FEELINGS statement. As you learn each new FLIP IT step, you will revisit these scenes and add to your responses. (Feel free to use creative license when interpreting the photos.) Sample responses appear in the back of this book in Appendix D.

**A child breaks crayons into pieces.**
- What would you say to address FEELINGS and set a LIMIT?

_____

_____

_____

 **A child crawls under the table during transition time.**
- What would you say to address FEELINGS and set a LIMIT?

_____

_____

_____

 **Children fight over the paintbrush.**
- What would you say to address FEELINGS and set a LIMIT?

_____

_____

_____

# Frequently Asked Questions About Step 2 LIMITS

**1. My natural instinct is to tell a child no. How can I unlearn this habit?**

Simply saying no, especially during dangerous times, is normal. As long as you acknowledge feelings first, an occasional "no" won't hurt. Stick to a few positive, simple rules that fit a variety of situations (for instance, "We use gentle touches").

**2. Is there ever a time when I can do FEELINGS, INQUIRIES, and PROMPTS (FIP) because a LIMIT is not necessary?**

During the FLIP IT process, you may do the FEELINGS step only to realize that a LIMIT is not necessary, but if the child is engaging in unhealthy coping, you may want to move toward problem solving. For example, if a child says, "I am so stupid," you may respond to FEELINGS by saying, "I can see you are feeling really frustrated by that puzzle." There may not necessarily be a LIMIT for feeling sad about yourself, in which case you can skip LIMITS and move forward to INQUIRIES and PROMPTS so that the child learns better coping skills. Some FLIP'ers may choose to set a LIMIT like, "I can see you are feeling really frustrated by that puzzle. We say good things about ourselves."

**3. The sample responses in this guide do not use the word "but" when delivering a LIMITS message. Why?**

It is very natural to say, "Yes, you are feeling angry, but we are friendly here." Using the word "but" after a FEELINGS statement negates the child's feelings. Most LIMITS statements can be delivered without taking away from the FEELINGS statement simply by leaving out the "but." Instead say, "Yes, you are feeling angry. We are friendly here."

**4. What if the child is nonverbal or developmentally delayed?**
All children need limits, but they should be appropriate to developmental levels and individual needs. What may be a limit for a child who is typically developing may not be a limit for a child with autism, Down syndrome, or other developmental delays. Keep in mind that even if a child cannot respond, it is important to talk about limits and expectations daily. You can narrate a child's challenging experiences by talking about feelings as well as limits. Keep talking, even if a child cannot or does not respond. The exercise of narrating often gives adults a better perspective on the situation and helps us see the challenges and the possibilities through the child's eyes. (See Appendix C.)

**5. What if different adults have different rules?**
When possible, share your positive, simple, and loving limits with the other adults in the child's life (teachers, family members, babysitters), and ask them to be your partners in consistency. When rules in different settings contradict each other and confuse the child, discuss and agree on a compromise that is in the child's best interest. Most children learn quickly how to distinguish between the expectations of different caregivers and environments. Be as consistent as you can be.

**6. What do I do if I end up having different limits for different children based on their abilities, needs, and ICK?**
It is appropriate to have a set of general limits (guidelines) that you apply to multiple children, but it is also appropriate to individualize. Every child is unique, and some may be better equipped to stay within our boundaries than others. For example, we may expect most children to attend circle time for 10 minutes, but we may only ask that a child with autism or a child with a lot of ICK try to join circle for two minutes before finding something quiet to do instead. Over the course of time, we may choose to increase our expectation for that child and set new limits as the child grows and develops skills. Limits are like goals, and we want to set achievable goals for each child. Adjusting limits based on abilities and needs is the fair thing to do, and fair does not mean everything must be equal. These adaptations teach children about diversity and tolerance, and you will find that most children are far more accepting of these differences than you may expect.

**7. What if the child gets really angry when I give a limit?**
Children might become angry when a limit is set because it is hard to live with. If the limit escalates the situation, return to a discussion of feelings ("I can see you are pretty angry about having to follow the rules"). Once you have returned to feelings, re-establish the limit and quickly move on to the INQUIRIES and PROMPTS steps. These steps let the child know you are going to try to help her find a way to live with the limit, then move forward to something more positive. If your attempts to talk it through continue to escalate the behavior, wait until the child is able to hear you.

# Step 2 LIMITS Promotes Resilience

Doing the LIMITS step with children helps to strengthen a child's attachment with adults. Loving limits send a message of caring and concern for children's well-being. When children know what is expected of them and that adults want to keep them safe, they begin to trust. Initiative is also strengthened during the LIMITS step. Limits help children know how, when, where, and with whom it is safe to explore the world. Children learn the most when they explore safely and fully. Finally, the LIMITS step strengthens a child's self-regulation. Limits help children better understand and engage in behaviors that society considers appropriate. Doing the LIMITS step now provides benefits that last forever.

The LIMITS step was inspired by a Devereux Center for Resilient Children (DCRC) resource that suggested setting limits with children. For more information on the Devereux Center for Resilient Children resources and materials see Appendix E.

# Notes

# 🔍 Step 3—INQUIRIES

*Michael (three years old) and Skyler (seven years old) have parents who have been FLIP'ing IT with them since they were born. I was always eager to babysit for these children because they were so easy! One night while I was babysitting Michael and Skyler, we were making valentines for their friends at school. A small conflict broke out when the children realized that they did not have enough fuzzy heart stickers for all of their friends. Michael was pulling them toward him and Skyler was grabbing them back. While my babysitter radar told me to jump in, I quickly stopped in my tracks when Michael turned to his sister and said, "Skyler, we have a problem, we both want these stickers. We shouldn't fight, so what should we do?" Skyler took a deep breath (clearly a seasoned and confident problem-solver) and suggested that they divide them up "one for you, one for me, until they are gone—and when they're gone, they're gone." Michael agreed to this solution. They dealt out the stickers and happily moved on.*

*FLIP IT can make life so much easier because children learn to solve problems on their own instead of needing us to put out the fires.*

*—Jessica, college student and babysitter (California)*

Once you have talked with a child about FEELINGS and LIMITS, move on to Step 3 INQUIRIES. Encourage children to think

33

about solutions to their challenges. Ask questions that promote problem-solving and healthy coping skills. Inquiries invite children to think, learn, and gain self-regulation.

## Why Do INQUIRIES Matter?

Inquiries are good questions that encourage children to think their way through challenging situations. When children feel overwhelmed by emotions and frustrated by limits, it is difficult for them to think and cope. They may shut down or act out. Fortunately, these challenges provide an opportunity to learn. For example, if Jacob grabs Taya's toy, she has the opportunity to learn how to get it back safely. To teach children to think and cope during times of challenge, we must give them a chance to solve the problem on their own. Asking the child to take part in finding a healthy solution lets her know you believe in her. ("What do you think you should do to get that toy back?")

## What Are Some Common FLOPs with This Step?

FLOPs happen when we step in too quickly to solve a child's problem for him. Although we may have good intentions, the child does not learn that he can solve problems himself. He does not learn to problem solve or how to find healthy coping options. He does not get the feeling of success or accomplishment that comes with using self-regulation. Adults who regularly solve problems for children often feel like firefighters going from one emergency to the next. Putting out fires all day is exhausting. Empowering children through inquiries teaches them to use their own fire extinguishers, so that they don't require you at every alarm.

Sometimes we FLOP when we ask a question with an intimidating, demanding, or unsupportive tone (for example, "What are you going to do next?" while tapping a toe or looking angry). Learning best takes place in the context of a safe and nurturing relationship. When children are learning to think and problem solve, they need encouragement. The tone of your inquiry should let the child know you believe in him and that you want him to succeed.

# Take Some Time to Reflect

1.   Inquiries work best when they are open-ended and spark critical thinking, creativity, and possibilities. In our eagerness, we sometimes ask leading questions that do not encourage thinking and can be answered with a simple yes or no. A closed or leading question, such as "Do you want to try the fork?" does little to inspire creative problem solving. A better open-ended inquiry might be "What do you think we can try?" Practice turning the leading questions below into open-ended inquiries.

Leading question: "Do you want to sit on my lap to feel safe?"
Open-ended inquiry: "What would make you feel safe right now?"

Leading question: "Do you think you should ask nicely?"
Open-ended inquiry: "What is a nice way to ask?"

Leading question: "Can you ask him to take turns?"
Open-ended inquiry: _____

Leading question: "Can you roll the car on the floor instead?"
Open-ended inquiry: _____

2.   To help you remember why the INQUIRIES step is so important, answer the following questions. Each one reinforces the value of helping children solve their own problems now, so the skill will last forever.

- Do I want children to feel confident that they can handle most conflicts?
  ☐Yes   ☐No

- Do I want children to be good problem-solvers?
  ☐Yes   ☐No

- Do I want children to ask questions that encourage thinking from others?
  ☐Yes   ☐No

- Do I want children to be able to think quickly and clearly in a crisis?
  ☐Yes   ☐No

- Do I want children to have healthy coping strategies when they feel ICK?
  ☐Yes   ☐No

Inquiries will strengthen the qualities reflected in these five questions.

# How do I get started with Step 3 INQUIRIES?

- *Change a habit.* Think to yourself, "How can I get the child to think?" Then ask an open-ended question that invites her to think about a solution.
- *Use some tools.* Use the practice pictures in this book and create your own reminder tools (posters, stickers, and bracelets) to help you get comfortable doing the INQUIRIES step.
- *Know when to move on.* In many cases, you will need to move on to PROMPTS fairly quickly because a child does not yet know how to problem solve without help. The goal is that you will only need the F, L, and I, not needing to move on to PROMPTS because the child solves the problem on her own.

## "What should I say?"

Below are sample lead-in phrases to engage a child during the INQUIRIES step. They may come in handy when you are first learning to FLIP IT. Choose some samples you like and then make them your own.

- "How do you think we can fix this?"
- "What could we do instead?"
- "Is there another way?"
- "How can we make this easier?"
- "What else could we do to get us there?"
- "What is a friendly way you could ____?"
- "What are we going to do to make this work?"
- "How could we make this fun?"

# Practice Pictures

Revisit the following photos and add an INQUIRIES question to your FEELINGS and LIMITS statements. As you learn each new FLIP IT step, you will revisit these scenes and add to your responses. (Feel free to use creative license when interpreting the photos.) Sample responses appear in Appendix D.

**A child breaks crayons into pieces.**
- Recall the FEELINGS and LIMITS statements and offer a question (INQUIRY) to encourage problem solving.

_____

_____

_____

**A child crawls under the table during transition time.**
- Recall the FEELINGS and LIMITS statements and offer a question (INQUIRY) to encourage problem solving.

_____

_____

_____

 **Children fight over the paintbrush.**
- Recall the FEELINGS and LIMITS statements and offer a question (INQUIRY) to encourage problem solving.

_____

_____

_____

# Frequently Asked Questions About Step 3 INQUIRIES

**1. What if I make an INQUIRY and the child does not respond?**
Most children will give you a blank stare the first few times you make an INQUIRY. If there is no imminent danger, let them think for a while before moving on to PROMPTS.

**2. How long should I wait for a child to think?**
The timing of your FLIP IT sequence will depend on the situation and the child involved. Children who do not have experience problem solving need to know you will support them by allowing time to think. As the child is thinking of possible solutions, you can be thinking of prompts to use, if needed.

**3. Can I use the INQUIRIES technique at other times?**
Certainly. Every situation presents multiple opportunities to invite a child to problem solve. The more children practice problem-solving skills, the better thinkers they will be during stressful and non-stressful times.

**4. What if I make an INQUIRY and the child's idea is not appropriate?**

Often children offer fantasy solutions or self-centered ideas. Compliment them for trying and refine your question so they can try again. ("Hmm … what else could we try that would be more fair?")

**5. How can I problem solve with a child who has limited or no language?**

When children have limited or no language skills, it is important to lend your voice to their problem-solving process. Voice the INQUIRIES step out loud to inspire your own creative thinking ("That noise is really loud and it looks like it's making you nervous. What can we do to help you with the noise?") This will help you think from the child's point of view when she can't tell you. (See Appendix C.)

**6. Should my INQUIRY be a question that leads to better coping skills around the feeling or the situation?**

For really intense feelings, the inquiry may focus more on coping with feelings instead of changing a particular situation. ("What can you do with that mad?") Sometimes addressing feelings in Step 1 is enough, and the inquiry will relate more to changing the situation. ("What can you do if you want more?") The child is likely to let you know if he needs more focus on his challenging feeling or quick help thinking through a challenging situation. Either direction helps. Trust that you will decide what is best for each unique situation and adjust when needed.

**7. What if I make an INQUIRY and the child's response is negative or hostile?**

Return to Step 1 FEELINGS. If a child begins to shut down or act out during your attempt to problem solve, remember she is new to identifying her feelings, living with limits, and finding healthy solutions. You might say, "I can see that my question has made you very angry, and you are yelling. We use friendly voices. How can we help you with your anger?"

# Step 3 INQUIRIES Promotes Resilience

Doing the INQUIRIES step strengthens children's attachments with adults. Asking children how to solve a problem conveys respect and trust. This process supports children's relationships with peers, teachers, and family members. Initiative is also strengthened during the INQUIRIES step by inspiring children to take on the world's challenges with confidence and by promoting their ability to think about long-term solutions. Finally, the INQUIRIES step strengthens a child's self-regulation. Children develop healthy coping skills that can last a lifetime when they are invited to participate in problem solving, rather than letting their bad feelings control their behavior. Doing the INQUIRIES step now provides benefits that last forever.

The INQUIRIES step was inspired by a Devereux Center for Resilient Children (DCRC) resource that suggested using problem-solving time with children. For more information on the Devereux Center for Resilient Children resources and materials see Appendix E.

# ⌂ STEP 4—PROMPTS

*As the mother of a child with special needs, I worry a lot about his future. I know life won't always be easy for him, and I don't want the world to run him over. Max is five years old, and his younger brother is already stronger and taking advantage of him. My instinct is to protect Max by swooping in and fixing all his problems, but I know I won't always be there to save him. The first time I tried FLIP IT was after Max had come crying to me that his brother had taken his pencil. My natural instinct would have been to get him a new pencil, but instead I said, "Honey, I know it is so frustrating when Jeremiah takes things from you. It makes you cry and come to me for help. You can help yourself (my new limit for Max). What could you say to Jeremiah to get your pencil back?" Of course he needed prompts, so I said, "Could you tell him with a strong voice that you want your pencil back?" He liked that idea and went back over to his brother and confidently said, "I want my pencil back!" Watching Max assert himself for the first time made me cry. I know that if I keep it up, Max will be a more empowered child and eventually a stronger adult.*

*—Ingrid, mother of five-year-old Max and three-year-old Jeremiah (New York)*

If the child is having difficulty problem solving after you have talked with her about FEELINGS and LIMITS and have made an INQUIRY, move on to Step 4 PROMPTS. Provide creative cues, clues, and suggestions for children having difficulty problem solving.

# Why Are PROMPTS Important?

Inquiries and open-ended questions do not always directly lead children to a solution. Some children lack experience with problem solving, while others may feel too overwhelmed with the challenge. It is difficult for them to imagine solutions. Prompts enable a problem-solver to see other possibilities. These creative cues, clues, and suggestions help children find their own answers. Prompts may involve sharing a personal example of how you have handled similar situations (for example, "When I get mad, I like to scribble on paper"). Some prompts are suggestions (such as "You might try using tape to put that back together"). Prompting can include asking leading questions (such as "Hmm, I wonder if we could try walking backward"). You also can offer the child some positive choices where both options are desirable (for example, "You could try warming your mittens on the heater or letting me put them in the dryer"). Use the child's strengths and interests to spark his creativity. Enthusiastic, bright ideas can lead the way to better problem-solving skills.

# What Are Some Common FLOPs with This Step?

FLOPs happen when we give up on finding a solution. Finding a solution to a problem requires patience, creativity, and commitment. When we keep trying to think of good ideas until we figure it out, we set a great example.

Sometimes we FLOP when we do not offer prompts with positivity or enthusiasm. Young children may need you to capture their attention as well as their imagination. If you sound excited and optimistic about the solution, the child is more likely to get on board.

# Take Some Time to Reflect

1. You can offer prompts in a variety of ways. Try some of the following methods for getting children excited about finding solutions.

- Use an example of how you have handled similar situations.
- Offer suggestions.
- Ask leading questions.
- Use the child's strengths and interests to spark his creativity.

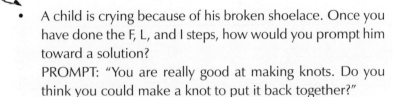

Practice offering prompts in the following scenarios:

- A child is crying because of his broken shoelace. Once you have done the F, L, and I steps, how would you prompt him toward a solution?
  PROMPT: "You are really good at making knots. Do you think you could make a knot to put it back together?"

- A child is hiding because she is scared of the hammering sound. Once you have done the F, L, and I steps, how would you prompt her toward a solution?
  PROMPT:

  _____

  _____

- A child is jumping on the furniture and getting very excited. Once you have done the F, L, and I steps, how would you prompt him toward a solution?
  PROMPT:

  _____

  _____

- A child is angry because she can't find her toy. Once you have done the F, L, and I steps, how would you prompt her toward a solution?
  PROMPT:

  _____

  _____

2.  Sometimes the answers to our problems are obvious, but follow-through is still difficult. For example, many people want to lose weight and know the answer is exercise and eating right, but that does not mean they have incorporated those skills into their daily lives. Prompts help people find creative ways to cope. The following scenarios present some common problems that adults face. Practice coming up with creative solutions.

- I am so tired, but I have to keep working. What is a creative (safe) option to help me cope?

_____

_____

_____

- I am stuck in traffic, and honking my horn isn't helping. What is a creative option to help me cope?

_____

_____

_____

- I take every precaution, but I am still nervous about my children getting the flu. What is a creative option to help me cope?

_____

_____

_____

Just like children, we all need a little creativity to help us carry out solutions to our problems and use healthy coping skills.

# How do I get started with Step 4 PROMPTS?

- *Get creative.* Light the way to a solution. Offer children tools such as questions or suggestions for fixing their own problems. Prompting requires creativity.
- *Practice in your own life.* Try looking for creative solutions to challenges in your own life and the lives of other adults. You soon will see that the possibilities are endless.
- *Sell solutions.* When you present possible solutions to children, make the solutions sound enticing. Enthusiasm can inspire many of us to move toward a solution, even if we were feeling stuck.
- *Use some tools.* Use the practice pictures in this book along with your reminder kit tools (posters, stickers, and bracelets) to help you get comfortable doing the PROMPTS step.

### "What should I say?"

Below are sample lead-in phrases pairing an inquiry with a prompt. They may come in handy when you are first learning to FLIP IT. Remember to personalize any sample you might use.

- "How do we think we can fix this? What could I get from my desk to help us put it back together?"
- "What do you think you could do instead? We could read or look for treasures in the room."
- "Is there another way? I bet we can think of a way to make that stronger with more, hmm … more what?"
- "What else could we do to get us there? Could we walk backward or hop on one foot?"
- "What is a friendly way we can ask each other? Maybe a lower voice?"
- "How are we going to make this fun?"

# Practice Pictures

Revisit the following photos and add a PROMPTS statement to your FEELINGS, LIMITS, and INQUIRY. (Feel free to use creative license when interpreting the photos.) Sample responses appear in Appendix D.

**A child breaks crayons into pieces.**
- Recall the FEELINGS, LIMITS, and INQUIRY and offer a PROMPT to help the child find a solution.

_____

_____

_____

 **A child crawls under the table during transition time.**
- Recall the FEELINGS, LIMITS, and INQUIRY and offer a PROMPT to help the child find a solution.

_____

_____

_____

 **Children fight over the paintbrush.**
- Recall the FEELINGS, LIMITS, and INQUIRY and offer a PROMPT to help the child find a solution.

_____

_____

_____

# Frequently Asked Questions About Step 4 PROMPTS

**1. What if I get stuck trying to be creative?**
Don't fear being silly. Sometimes the way out of a tough spot is humor. No one wants to be stuck, and a silly idea may be just what is needed to shift gears. You may also benefit from looking at the situation through the eyes of a child. Ask yourself, "If I was five, what would make me feel better?"

**2. What is the difference between an INQUIRY and a leading-question PROMPT?**

Inquiries are open-ended questions that encourage children to think without adult direction. If a child is unable to generate ideas on her own, move on to the PROMPTS step. Prompts are leading questions that point the child in a positive direction but still encourage her to make her own decisions. This process helps her take ownership of the solution.

**3. What if I don't think I can do this step?**

Practice! Practice! Practice! Offering prompts can be the hardest of the four steps. It requires the ability to think on your feet, which only gets better with practice.

**4. Can I use props to prompt?**

Absolutely! Use your environment and anything you can get your hands on to guide a child toward a solution (for example, puppets, toys, even pots and pans). Children sometimes need to see it before they can imagine it, so while you are prompting a child, offer visual cues. For example, while holding a box and nodding your head toward it, say, "Hmmm … I wonder where we could put your castle for safekeeping."

**5. How can I problem solve and suggest prompts with a child who has limited or no language?**

When a child has limited or no language, it is important to lend your voice to his problem-solving process. If you are trying to help a child who struggles with behavior, use the INQUIRIES and PROMPTS steps out loud with yourself to inspire your own creative thinking (for example, "That noise is really loud and it looks like it's bothering you. What can we do to help you with the noise? I wonder if some headphones with music would help"). This will help you think from the child's point of view, even when he cannot tell you. (See Appendix C.)

**6. What if the child does not respond to any of my prompts?**
Don't give up! One size does not fit all, and you may need to keep trying. Often a child does not respond to the prompts you offer because they differ from his negative choices. A child who feels very overwhelmed by the challenge before him may not accept any of your prompts, at which point you should start back at Step 1 FEELINGS ("It doesn't seem like you like any of the options I suggested. You must be feeling really stuck.")

# Step 4 PROMPTS Promotes Resilience

Doing the PROMPTS step with children strengthens their attachments with adults. Prompting children who feel stuck in their problem-solving efforts helps them feel that they are not alone and that they are supported by a special adult. Initiative is also strengthened during the PROMPTS step. Offering prompts helps children see possibilities; it encourages creativity and outside-the-box thinking that builds their confidence for future problem solving. Finally, the PROMPTS step strengthens a child's self-regulation. Prompts can provide children with opportunities to see the positive choices available to them. Doing the PROMPTS step now provides benefits that last forever.

The PROMPTS step was inspired by a Devereux Center for Resilient Children (DCRC) resource that suggested the technique of scaffolding children's learning. For more information on the DCRC resources and materials see Appendix E.

# Conclusion

**Life is a journey and each one of us has a suitcase that we take along for the ride. Hopefully, we have what we need in our suitcase when we hit a bump or break down. As adults, we are** important role models in a child's life. Reflect on what social and emotional skills you want a child to have at the ready when she faces a challenge in her life. Know that every challenge a child faces now is practice for what may come. Using FLIP IT helps us turn difficult times into teachable moments and opportunities to learn. FLIP IT helps instill life-long habits of identifying feelings, setting limits, asking good questions, and finding creative solutions. We hope you find FLIP IT an effective approach for helping children identify and cope with feelings in the context of a loving and safe relationship.

# Notes

# Appendix A:
# Literature Review

## ICK and CHALLENGING BEHAVIOR

- A variety of child and family risk factors contribute to early onset conduct disorders, which lead to more recalcitrant and intractable problem behaviors as the child develops. Some of those risk factors include lack of prenatal care, low birth weight, maternal depression, early temperament difficulties in infants, developmental disabilities, early behavior and adjustment problems, and inconsistent and harsh parenting. [Huffman, L. C., Mehlinger, S. L., & Kerivan, A. S. (2000). *Risk factors for academic and behavioral problems at the beginning of school.* Bethesda, MD: National Institute of Mental Health.]

- Children often experience negative emotions much more frequently than others and in response to a wider range of interpersonal situations. These frequent expressions and experiences place them at risk for social maladjustment. Anger arousal, for example, tends to motivate aggressive behavior, and frequent aggressive behavior marks the primary reason children dislike particular peers. [Williams, S. C., Lochman, J. E., & Phillips, N. C. (2003). Aggressive and nonaggressive boys' physiological and cognitive processes in response to peer provocations.

*Journal of Clinical Child and Adolescent Psychology, 32,* 568–576.]

- Inefficient emotion regulation physiologically inhibits a child's use of higher order cognitive processes (for example, working memory, attention, and planning) in the classroom. [Blair, C. (2002). School readiness: Integrating cognition and emotion in a neurobiological conceptualization of children's functioning at school entry. *American Psychologist, 57*(2), 111–127.]
- Challenging behaviors of young children do not simply fade away but, in many cases, continue to impact the child's development and social competence for many years. [Arnold, D. H., Ortiz, C., Curry, J. C., Stowe, R. M., Goldstein, N. E., Fisher, P. H., et al. (1999). Promoting academic success and preventing disruptive behavior disorders through community partnership. *Journal of Community Psychology, 27*, 589–598.]

## FEELINGS

- Emotional competence is central to children's ability to interact and form relationships. [Saarni, C. (1990). Emotional competence. In R. Thompson (Ed.), *Nebraska symposium: Socioemotional development* (pp. 115–161). Lincoln: University of Nebraska Press.]
- Talking about emotions helps young children understand their feelings. [Brown, J. R., & Dunn, J. (1996). Continuities in emotion understanding from three to six years. *Child Development, 67*(3), 789–803.]
- Researchers found that preschool-aged children better understand their feelings when adults explain emotions. [Denham, S. A., Zoller, D., & Couchoud, E. A. (1994). Socialization of preschoolers' emotion understanding. *Developmental Psychology, 30*(6), 928–937.]
- The ability to regulate the expression of anger is linked to an understanding of the emotion, and young children's ability to reflect on their anger is somewhat limited; therefore, young children need guidance from teachers and parents in understanding and managing their feelings of anger. [Zeman, J., &

Shipman, K. (1996). Children's expression of negative affect: Reasons and methods. *Developmental Psychology, 32*(5), 842–850.]

- When children have the ability to label emotions, they have a key skill with which to regulate emotions because they have experience in attaching a label to feelings inside and therefore can bring feelings to consciousness. [Greenburg, M. T., DeKlyen, M., & Speltz, M. L. (1989). *The relationship of insecure attachment to externalizing behavior problems in the preschool years.* Paper presented at the Society for Research in Child Development, Kansas City.]

- Parents influence children's emotional development through discussion of emotion, their reactions to children's emotions, and family expressiveness. Discussing emotions may explicitly teach children ways of understanding and managing emotional experiences. Emotion discussions can also help children learn to use emotion language and encourage emotion understanding. [Eisenberg, N., Cumberland, A., & Spinrad, T. (1998). Parental socialization of emotion. *Psychological Inquiry, 9,* 241–273.]

## LIMITS

- Research suggests that classrooms are well-managed when teachers provide clear, firm rules and a high level of monitoring and when they follow a set of simple, behaviorally oriented steps to minimize children's disruptive behavior. [Bear, G. G. (1998). School discipline in the United States: Prevention, correction, and long-term social development. *School Psychology Review, 27,* 14–32.]

- Treatment studies in which children of parents taught to provide clear, firm, calm, appropriate, and consistent limits and discipline exhibited decreased rates of misbehavior. [Kazdin, A. E. (1987). *Conduct disorder in childhood and adolescence.* Newbury Park, CA: SAGE.]

- Parenting practices associated with the development of conduct problems include inconsistent and harsh discipline and low nurturing. [Patterson, G. R., & Dishion, T. J. (1985). Contributions of families and peers to delinquency. *Criminology, 23,* 63–79.]

# INQUIRIES

- Optimal social-emotional growth is a function of attention being paid to nurturing relationships and instructional guidance that directs the young child toward prosocial competence and away from challenging behaviors. [Fox, L., Dunlap, G., Hemmeter, M. L., Joseph, G. E., & Strain, P. S. (2003, July). The teaching pyramid: A model for supporting social competence and preventing challenging behavior in young children. *Young Children,* 48–52.]
- A child who can consider alternative solutions to problems is less likely to, for example, push another child away simply because that child is in the way of a desired goal. [Pettit, G. S., Dodge, K. A. & Brown, M. M. (1988). Early family experience, social problem-solving patterns, and children's social competence. *Child Development, 59,* 107–120.]
- Observation of parent–child interaction in developmentally appropriate problem-solving situations is a common means of assessing the competence of children from infancy through middle childhood. [Elicker, J., Englund, M., & Sroufe, L. A. (1992). Predicting peer competence and peer relationships in childhood from early parent-child relationships. In R. Parke & G. Ladd (Eds.), *Family-peer relationships: Modes of linkage* (pp. 77–106). Hillsdale, NJ: Erlbaum.]
- Inefficient emotion regulation physiologically inhibits a child's use of higher order cognitive processes (e.g., working memory, attention, and planning) in the classroom. [Blair, C. (2002). School readiness: Integrating cognition and emotion in a neurobiological conceptualization of children's functioning at school entry. *American Psychologist, 57*(2), 111–127.]
- Children who thrive in social interactions with peers, particularly those who succeed in negative interactions, effectively

regulate their own emotions and subsequent emotion-related behaviors. [Denham, S. A., Blair, K. A., Schmidt, M., & DeMulder, E. (2002). Compromised emotional competence. Seeds of violence sown early? *American Journal of Orthopsychiatry, 72,* 70–82.]

# PROMPTS

- Teaching young children skills that can be used to replace challenging behaviors is one of the most effective, scientifically based interventions available for these behaviors. [Conroy, M. A., Dunlap, G., Clarke, S., & Alter, P. J. (2005). A descriptive analysis of behavioral intervention research with young children with challenging behavior. *Topics in Early Childhood Special Education, 25,* 157–166.]
- Optimal social–emotional growth is a function of attention being paid to nurturing relationships and instructional guidance that directs the young child toward prosocial competence and away from challenging behaviors. [Fox, L., Dunlap, G., Hemmeter, M. L., Joseph, G. E., & Strain, P. S. (2003, July). The teaching pyramid: A model for supporting social competence and preventing challenging behavior in young children. *Young Children,* 48–52.]
- Teaching children social skills, problem-solving, and anger-management strategies is effective for reducing conduct problems. [Kazdin, A. E., Siegel, J. C., & Bass, D. (1992). Cognitive problem-solving skills training and parent management training in the treatment of antisocial behavior in children. *Journal of Consulting and Clinical Psychology, 60,* 733–747.]
- Well-presented stories about emotions validate children's feelings and give information about anger. [Jalongo, M. (1986). Using crisis-oriented books with young children. In J. B. McCracken (Ed.), *Reducing stress in young children's lives,* (pp. 41–46). Washington, DC: NAEYC.]
- Children with better emotion regulation skills have been found to display greater social competence, better social skills, and

greater peer popularity. [Dunn, J., & Brown, J. (1994). Affect expression in the family, children's understanding of emotions, and their interactions with others. *Merrill-Palmer Quarterly, 40*(1), 120–137.]

NOTE: Literature review provided by Kristen Tenney-Blackwell.

# Appendix B: FLIP IT Activities to Use with Children

## ♡ FEELINGS Activities

- Invite children to draw a picture of how they feel when working through a problem and trying to use FLIP IT.
- Lead children in a drawing activity at group times. The teacher and/or children can draw faces that represent the feelings of different characters in a story.
- Have children cut pictures of faces from magazines and then tape them to poster board. Work with the children to label the facial expressions.
- Take pictures of the children expressing various emotions and tape the photos to poster board. Refer to them when discussing feelings.
- Focus on a "feeling of the week." Draw a picture of the face, write the word, and have each child take a turn drawing a face showing the emotion.

##  LIMITS Activities

- Work with children to create three simple, positively worded class rules. Write and post the rules in the classroom. When enforcing limits, refer to the rules you created together.
- Draw a stop sign on poster board and engage children in a discussion of behaviors that you don't want to see or hear in the classroom.
- Focus on a rule the group has difficulty following. Practice following the rule during a non-stressful time. For example, if children struggle with cleanup, create a cleanup game where you collect objects from around the room and each child has to race to put them away.
- Engage children in a discussion about why a rule is in place. Write the children's thoughts on poster board.
- Work with children to rewrite "stop" behaviors, such as "stop running," in more positive language, such as "walk." You will be surprised at how quickly the children can adapt to saying things in a more positive manner.

##  INQUIRIES Activities

- Post pictures from the FLIP IT flash card pictures on the wall with a large question mark under each picture. Engage children in a discussion about what they think they could do to solve the problem shown in the picture. Address a new picture card each week, and use picture cards from other resources, such as the *Second Step®* curriculum.
- Post a picture of a lightbulb and record (write and draw pictures of) good ideas (solutions) you hear and observe throughout the day. Review these with the children as a group so everyone can benefit from these teachable moments.
- When you are reading a story and a character has a problem, write or draw a picture of that problem. Then ask the children how they would solve it, and record their answers or ask them to draw a picture of their solutions.
- Post a "Question/Problem of the Day," such as "I want to play with my friends and don't know how." You also could cut a

picture from a magazine or draw a picture depicting this scenario. Present the problem at group time and ask the children to come up with ideas, writing or drawing pictures of their solutions. Review the ideas as a group.

- Hold a discussion with the children about what to do when they are stuck and can't think of a good way to solve a problem. The children may come up with some good ideas to use yourself!

 # PROMPTS Activities

- Write the words "How can we fix this?" on a poster with pictures of children being kind to each other (better yet, use pictures of the children you work with whenever possible). Whenever you are using FLIP IT and a child needs a visual cue, point to the poster and start to draw pictures or write words together that might work toward a solution.
- As a group, brainstorm solutions and ideas such as "ask an adult for help," "take turns," "set a timer for fair amounts of time for all," "share it together," and so forth. Write or draw these solutions on index cards and place them in a small bag. Keep the bag and some reusable adhesive near a poster board. When faced with a challenge and in need of prompts, pull two prompts from the bag and stick them to the poster board with the adhesive. Read the prompts aloud and ask the child which one of these ideas might work.
- Post a picture of a phone on the wall along with a list of the children in the class. When a child is stuck, refer to the picture of the phone and choose the name of a friend to call for help in coming up with a good solution. This is a good way to make all children feel valued and empowers them to work with each other in times of need.
- Ask the children to come up with three solutions that will work in almost every situation (for example, take a break, take a turn, talk about how you feel). List the three solutions on poster board or draw a picture of each solution. When working with a child and finding yourself in need of a prompt, look at the board and review the three solutions to see if any will work.

- Use poster board to illustrate the thought process involved in coming up with a good idea. When reading stories or working through teachable moments with the children, write or draw your first thought, then talk about why it will work or why it won't work. Use that solution or cross it out and try another. Explain to children that we don't always pick the best idea first, but sometimes, even as adults, we have to try a lot of different ways until we come up with a good answer.

NOTE: Suggestions provided by Karen Cairone, M.Ed., Devereux Center for Resilient Children.

# References

Copple, C., & Bredekamp, S. (Eds). (2009). *Developmentally appropriate practice in early childhood programs* (3rd ed). Washington, DC: NAEYC.

Gartrell, D. (2004). *The power of guidance: Teaching social-emotional skills in early childhood classrooms*. Ontario, Canada: Thomson/Delmar Learning.

Hyson, M. (2004). *The emotional development of young children*. New York, NY: Teachers College Press.

Hyson, M. (2008). *Enthusiastic and engaged learners: Approaches to learning in the early childhood classroom*. New York, NY: Teachers College Press.

Kaiser, B., & Rasminsky, J. S. (2007). *Challenging behavior in young children: Understanding, preventing, and responding effectively* (2nd ed.). Boston, MA: Allyn & Bacon.

Levin, D. E. (2003). *Teaching young children in violent times: Building a peaceable classroom* (2nd ed.). Washington, DC: NAEYC.

# Appendix C: Adapting FLIP IT for Individual Children's Needs

**The FLIP IT strategy is designed for all children. Nevertheless, you might have some special considerations and need to adapt it or individualize it for some** children. We offer examples here. We welcome additional feedback on using FLIP IT with a child who needs adaptations. Please share your ideas with us at www.moreflipit.org, so we can best support every child in his or her ability to develop resilience and learn to problem solve.

## ♡ FEELINGS Adaptations

- When working with children with limited verbal skills, try using feelings posters, feelings faces, and feelings wheels. Children can see a variety of emotions and choose which one applies to how they feel.
- To reinforce concepts in a fun and repetitive way, read books and play music that involve labeling and discussing feelings.
- To help children who have difficulty reading facial expressions and associating them with the labeled feeling, an adult can mimic the facial expression of someone who is sad, angry, frustrated, and so on, and show this face to the child as they gently talk through what her face is showing.

- Try using mirrors (when culturally appropriate) to help children realize how their faces and bodies express strong emotions.
- Use techniques such as breathing to music tempo, belly breathing, yoga, and so forth to help children focus on the excitement in their bodies when they are feeling strong emotions.

#  LIMITS Adaptations

- To help children learn how to most safely play and learn together, provide visual and pictorial displays of classroom rules and expectations.
- Remind children when they use a behavior that may be harmful or unacceptable in the learning environment by using a small stop sign or a thumbs down, or slowly shaking your head side to side.
- When there is a limit or rule that needs to be enforced, a cue or gentle touch from the caregiver may help a child who is easily distracted.

#  INQUIRIES Adaptations

- Open-ended questions are ideal but not applicable to every child and every learner. When a child is limited in the decision-making process and/or verbal skills, adults may need to ask simple yes-or-no questions to guide a child toward a solution.
- A child with limited reasoning abilities may benefit from having the adult reason aloud to consistently provide examples of the reasoning process. ("Let's see, if Rhianna gets a turn first and Mary has to wait, is that fair? No, Mary did have the toy first. What if Mary had it first and then gave it to Rhianna after 1 minute? Does that seem more fair?")
- Children who are unable to come up with any potential solutions on their own may be able to choose between two simple solutions. Offer two choices so the child can feel like she helped find the solution.

# PROMPTS Adaptations

- Try using props. Children may be more agreeable to trying ideas offered by a soft bunny puppet rather than those offered by a teacher who seems like an expert with all the answers.
- To help children who are limited in cognitive ability, try creating a basket of good idea cards. A child and teacher can pull one out together and consider whether it might be of use. For example, a good idea card could include a photograph of two children sharing a toy and the word "share." A teacher and child could discuss whether the good idea would work in a specific situation.
- For a child with special needs, invite the other children to offer encouragement, which reinforces successful use of a solution and empowers the child to work through the challenge the next time.

NOTE: Suggestions provided by Karen Cairone, M.Ed., Devereux Center for Resilient Children.

# References

Bell, S. H., Carr, V., Denno, D., Johnson, L. J., & Phillips, L. R. (2004). *Challenging behaviors in early childhood settings: Creating a place for all children.* Baltimore, MD: Paul H. Brookes.

Gartrell, D. (2004). *The power of guidance: Teaching social-emotional skills in early childhood classrooms.* Ontario, Canada: Thomson/Delmar Learning.

Hyson, M. (2008). *Enthusiastic and engaged learners: Approaches to learning in the early childhood classroom.* New York, NY: Teachers College Press.

Riley, D., San Juan, R. R., Klinkner, J., & Ramminger, A. (2008). *Social and emotional development: Connecting science and practice in early childhood settings.* St. Paul, MN: Redleaf Press.

Sandall, S., & Ostrosky, M. (1999). Practical ideas for addressing challenging behaviors. *Young Exceptional Children MONograph Series.* Denver, CO: The Division for Early Childhood of the Council for Exceptional Children.

Smith, C. J. (2008). *Behavioral challenges in early childhood settings.* St. Paul, MN: Redleaf Press.

# Appendix D:
# Practice Pictures

The photographs on the following pages show children engaging in a variety of challenging behaviors.

1. Flip through the challenging behavior scenarios found in these photos.
2. Practice what you would say in each scenario by using the four FLIP IT steps.
3. You should interpret the photo using your imagination and creative license. Give the children names, make up the back story, or even give the child in the photo the personality characteristics of a child you know well.
4. There are many possible ways to FLIP each scenario based on your interpretation of the photo. The sample responses are only one of several appropriate ways to respond to the situation.

# 1. Breaking crayons into little pieces
## "What should I say?"

 1. **FEELINGS:**

_____

_____

 2. **LIMITS:**

_____

_____

 3. **INQUIRIES:**

_____

_____

 4. **PROMPTS:**

_____

_____

# 1. Breaking crayons into little pieces
## "What should I say?"

 1. **FEELINGS**:

"I see that you are breaking crayons and your face looks really mad."

 2. **LIMITS**:

"You are allowed to break our 'old' crayons when you are feeling mad."

 3. **INQUIRIES**:

"What would you like to do to get your mad out?"

 4. **PROMPTS**:

"We could find the old crayons or we could try breaking sticks."

## Notes

_____
_____
_____
_____
_____
_____
_____
_____
_____
_____
_____
_____
_____
_____

## 2. Crawling under the table during transition time

"What should I say?"

 1. **FEELINGS:**

_____

_____

 2. **LIMITS:**

_____

_____

 3. **INQUIRIES:**

_____

_____

 4. **PROMPTS:**

_____

_____

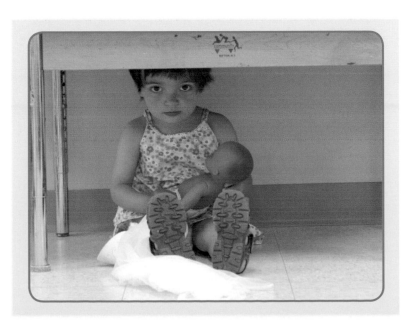

# 2. Crawling under the table during transition time

### "What should I say?"

 1. **FEELINGS**:

"I see that you are under the table and you look worried."

 2. **LIMITS**:

"Everyone needs to help clean up."

 3. **INQUIRIES**:

"How can you clean up and still feel safe?"

 4. **PROMPTS**:

"Do you want to be my cleanup helper and stay close to me?"

## Notes

_____
_____
_____
_____
_____
_____
_____
_____
_____
_____
_____
_____
_____
_____
_____
_____
_____
_____

## 3. Fighting over the paintbrush
### "What should I say?"

 1. **FEELINGS:**

_____

_____

 2. **LIMITS:**

_____

_____

 3. INQUIRIES:

_____

_____

 4. PROMPTS:

_____

_____

# 3. Fighting over the paintbrush
## "What should I say?"

 1. **FEELINGS**:
"I see that you both really want that paintbrush and you are starting to grab."

 2. **LIMITS**:
"We use our words when we want something."

 3. **INQUIRIES**:

"How could you both get a paintbrush?"

 4. **PROMPTS**:

"I bet there is a grown-up in the room who knows where to find more paintbrushes if you ask."

## Notes

_____
_____
_____
_____
_____
_____
_____
_____
_____
_____
_____
_____
_____
_____
_____
_____
_____

## 4. Throwing a ball inside when it is against the rules

"What should I say?"

 1. **FEELINGS**:

_____

_____

 2. **LIMITS**:

_____

_____

 3. INQUIRIES:

_____

_____

4. PROMPTS:

_____

_____

## 4. Throwing a ball inside when it is against the rules

"What should I say?"

  1. **FEELINGS**:

"You look like you are having so much fun throwing that ball. It must be hard to stop."

  2. **LIMITS**:

"We throw balls outside."

  3. **INQUIRIES**:

"What can you throw inside that is safe?"

  4. **PROMPTS**:

"Is there anything soft in this room that would be safer?"

## Notes

_____
_____
_____
_____
_____
_____
_____
_____
_____
_____
_____
_____
_____

# 5. Threatening to cause harm
## "What should I say?"

 1.  **FEELINGS:**

_____

_____

 2.  **LIMITS:**

_____

_____

 3.  INQUIRIES:

_____

_____

 4.  PROMPTS:

_____

_____

## 5. Threatening to cause harm
### "What should I say?"

1. **FEELINGS**:

   "Your words are telling me that you are SO mad."

2. **LIMITS**:

   "We are peaceful here. We don't hurt or kill."

3. **INQUIRIES**:

   "What can we do to help you with how angry you are feeling?"

4. **PROMPTS**:

   "Would you like to scribble all over the paper or squeeze some play-dough?"

## Notes

_____
_____
_____
_____
_____
_____
_____
_____
_____
_____
_____
_____
_____
_____
_____
_____
_____
_____

# 6. Child is saying, "I'm so stupid!"

### "What should I say?"

 1. **FEELINGS**:

_____

_____

 2. **LIMITS**:

_____

_____

 3. INQUIRIES:

_____

_____

4. PROMPTS:

_____

_____

# 6. Child is saying, "I'm so stupid!"
## "What should I say?"

 1. **FEELINGS**:

"You must be feeling pretty sad inside to say that about yourself."

 2. **LIMITS**:

"We say good things about ourselves."

 3. **INQUIRIES**:

"What can you do when you are feeling sad inside?"

 4. **PROMPTS**:

"You could sing, 'I can do it' to yourself, or you could ask for help."

## Notes

_____
_____
_____
_____
_____
_____
_____
_____
_____
_____
_____
_____
_____
_____
_____
_____
_____
_____

# 7. Refusing to clean up
## "What should I say?"

 1. **FEELINGS**:

_____

_____

 2. **LIMITS**:

_____

_____

 3. INQUIRIES:

_____

_____

 4. PROMPTS:

_____

_____

## 7. Refusing to clean up
### "What should I say?"

 1. **FEELINGS**:

"I can see that you really do not want to clean up right now. You were having fun with the cars."

 2. **LIMITS**:

"It is cleanup time for all the boys and girls."

 3. **INQUIRIES**:

"Where could we save this car so that you can use it later?"

 4. **PROMPTS**:

"I could put it in my pocket or in the 'save it' box for you to use later."

## Notes

_____
_____
_____
_____
_____
_____
_____
_____
_____
_____
_____
_____
_____
_____
_____
_____

# 8. Throwing toys to cause harm

*(Remember, if there is immediate danger, set the LIMIT first!)*

## "What should I say?"

 1. **FEELINGS**:

_____

_____

 2. **LIMITS**:

_____

_____

 3. **INQUIRIES**:

_____

_____

 4. **PROMPTS**:

_____

_____

# 8. Throwing toys to cause harm

*(Remember, if there is immediate danger, set the LIMIT first!)*

## "What should I say?"

1. **LIMITS**:

   "No throwing toys, we keep each other safe!" (Get your hands on the block if you can.)

2. **FEELINGS**:

   "I can see that you are getting very mad with your friend and you are throwing toys."

3. INQUIRIES:

   "What can you do when you are mad at a friend?"

4. PROMPTS:

   "Instead of hurting your friend when you are mad, you tell him with your brave voice, 'I am mad because you are sitting too close to me. Please scoot over.'"

## Notes

_____
_____
_____
_____
_____
_____
_____
_____
_____
_____
_____
_____
_____

# Appendix E: Devereux Center for Resilient Children

All Devereux Center for Resilient Children (DCRC) resources are based on six principles related to building resilience.

- The strengths, happiness, and resilience of all children: DCRC recognizes that all children, no matter their current risk status, need a strong social and emotional foundation.
- Strong partnerships between parents and child-serving professionals: DCRC recognizes that parents and caregivers with consistent, nurturing, developmentally appropriate expectations of children are critical to their social and emotional health.
- Collaboration to optimize positive outcomes: All adults in the life of a child working together to provide consistent, positive care to young children is tremendously beneficial to promoting within-child protective factors.
- The well-being of the adults who parent, nurture, and educate children: Young children's healthy social and emotional development is dependent on the health and well-being of the adults who care for them.

- Strength-based approaches: Research confirms that promoting children's social and emotional strengths reduces the development and escalation of behavioral concerns.
- Data-driven decision making: Decisions about how to optimize a child's social and emotional health must be based on reliable and valid information. The DCRC approach uses data to inform decisions and also to track progress.

# References

Koralek, D. (1999). *The Devereux Early Childhood Assessment— Classroom strategies to promote children's social and emotional development.* Lewisville, NC: Kaplan.

Koralek, D. (1999). *The Devereux Early Childhood Assessment— For now and forever; A guide for families on promoting social and emotional development.* Lewisville, NC: Kaplan.

LeBuffe, P. A., & Naglieri, J. A. (1999). *Devereux Early Childhood Assessment (DECA), technical manual, and user's guide.* Lewisville, NC: Kaplan.

# Appendix F: Research Supports FLIP IT®

A thorough review of the literature informed the development of the FLIP IT® strategy, ensuring that each of the steps comprising the technique is based on solid evidence for how to best support young children's social and emotional development (See Appendix A: Literature Review).

In 2016, a longitudinal empirical evaluation of the effectiveness of FLIP IT® was completed to validate its ability to systematically and consistently produce positive outcomes over an extended period of time. The primary goal of the empirical evaluation was to determine the effectiveness of the FLIP IT® parent-training program in decreasing negative social, emotional, and behavioral outcomes and in increasing positive social, emotional, and behavioral outcomes among participants' children. In the study conducted by Miami University's Center for School-Based Mental Health Programs, parents of young children (n=321) were trained to use the FLIP IT® strategy. On the 321 participants, data were collected at baseline (before receiving the FLIP IT training) and at three post-training follow-up time points (immediately following training, 3 months later, and 6+ months later). Based on the results of this evaluation, the FLIP IT® parent-training model appears to be an effective parenting method for:
- decreasing children's behavior problems, anxiety, depression, withdrawal, somatic complaints, delinquent behavior, aggressive behavior, and developmental problems; and
- increasing children's abilities to use independent thought and action to meet their needs (initiative), to express emotions and manage behaviors in healthy ways (self-regulation), and to promote and maintain mutual, positive connections with other children and adults (attachment/relationships).

In addition, the FLIP IT steps appear to be an effective parenting method for decreasing inconsistent or permissive parenting strategies, harsh or punitive parenting strategies, parent/caregiver distress levels, dysfunctional interactions within the parent-child relationship, and parental beliefs that their child(ren) is (are) difficult to manage.

In focus groups and interviews, parents/caregivers described being overwhelmingly satisfied with their overall FLIP IT experience. To read the executive summary or full research report, visit www.moreflipit.org

# About the Author

Rachel Wagner, MSW, is a lead national trainer and early childhood mental-health specialist for the Devereux Center for Resilient Children. She is the author of *FLIP IT!® Transforming Challenging Behavior* and coauthor of *Your Journey Together: Building the Resilience of Children and Families*.

Most recently Rachel has coauthored the Devereux Resilient Leadership Survey to support resilient leadership practices. Rachel travels the country speaking to groups on topics related to social-emotional health, resilience, and the connection to trauma-sensitive practices. She also provides national webinars, technical assistance, and reflective supervision to mental-health professionals coping with secondary trauma. Rachel has more than twenty years of experience working with children with diverse backgrounds and needs.

Rachel began her career as a preschool teacher and then worked as a teacher and counselor in a therapeutic preschool. She also served as an early childhood mental-health coordinator and consultant for several Head Start programs. Later, She began one of New York's first early childhood mental-health consultation services.

Rachel currently resides in the Syracuse, NY, area with her family. She is a passionate speaker, a dedicated listener, and an advocate for children who communicate in unique ways.

## FLIP IT!® Online Course, 2nd Edition

Parents and professionals interested in learning more about the FLIP IT strategy may want to experience the FLIP IT Online Course. The entire length of the course is approximately 2.5 hours and includes opportunities to interact, reflect, apply skills, and assess your understanding of the strategy with a final assessment (optional for parents). This self-paced course, narrated by Rachel Wagner, can be taken module by module or all at one time. Empower yourself and your colleagues by taking this course today!
Item # 90146
www.kaplanco.com